The Bright White Tree

THE BRIGHT WHITE TREE

JOANNA SELDON

First published in 2017 by
Worple Press
Achill Sound, 2b Dry Hill Road
Tonbridge
Kent TN9 1LX.
www.worplepress.co.uk

Cover image: Louise James

Printed by imprintdigital
Upton Pyne, Exeter
www.imprintdigital.com

Typeset and cover design by narrator typesetters and designers
www.narrator.me.uk
info@narrator.me.uk
033 022 300 39

ISBN: 978-1-905208-38-8

Acknowledgements and Notes

Joanna's poetry, as well as the text of speeches, three novels and several short stories, can be found on her website: www.joannaseldon.co.uk.

'The Blossom Falls' will appear in a Worple Press anthology of poems on trees in collaboration with The Woodland Trust to celebrate the Woodland Charter. Further details can be found on www.worplepress.co.uk.

Other poems will appear in *Agenda*, *The North* and *The Daily Telegraph*: thanks to the editors.

Anthony Seldon said on BBC Radio 4's *Desert Island Discs* that if he could have one luxury item on the island, it would be a collection of Joanna's poetry.

This is it.

Contents

Renewal

I wrote this short poem during a stay in hospital. I woke up one morning to find that the scaffolding blocking out the window had been removed. Time in hospital can have its good moments.

Early morning – and I heard
The men shout, and the clanging
Crash of lopped
Scaffolding.

Now, as I open
Curtains and blinds, I see
Light before it is mine,
And the day comes

Bursting in
With a view.
A view!

Redbrick buildings
Trimmed with white,
Church spire a rocket
To heaven, trees awaiting
Spring splatter of leaves,
The tops of Fulham Road buses
And the first sky
For five days

The world is still there.

I switch on my iPod to find
This day starting
With my song.
So I partner my drip machine
And dance
To
The Flying Pickets.

Day.

Robin In York

The Minster bell has just tolled twelve
As I pause on the city wall to take in
This chill late January Sunday morning.
The Minster's skirts slope green already
With spring, and the promise of later bluebells.
Clumps of snowdrops cling to the banks.

And, straight ahead of me, so close
I could reach to try and touch a feather,
A robin sits on a stump and pauses with me.
The head swivels a little, eyes alert,
But he doesn't seem to fear me.
I can see the pulse of his heart,
The throb pressing the red throat.
I can see the tiny, silver cloud
Where his breath meets the cold air.
Do birds, chill-blooded, have warm breath?
Perhaps the cloud I see is mine.

On The Beach At St Andrew's

Wind drives dust of fine sand across the beach;
Setting sun turns sand into streams of light,
Ribbons of bright light flowing down the beach.
They rush seawards, always rush to the sea.
So we are dust, sunlit dust scurrying
For the uncharted sea, to merge and melt.

Christmas Day 2012: Brighton Beach

Crunch of pebbles – clean and sharp
As this cold blue winter sky
And your new red scarf tugging

In the wind. We are alone –
Imagine indoor people
Still picking on turkey –

But we have come with a gift
And stand, braced against the wind,
Unlidding the wooden box

As if we were the Magi.
This does indeed hold treasure.
You puncture the bag; the wind

Snatches its gift. And now,
Like smoke, the precious ashes
Stream along the beach, just as

Not long ago, Toby ran,
The crashing sea in his ears,
As the puppy longs to do.

Pavilion Haiku

White light bleaches
Boats and buildings
    Beige and grey,
    Fixed by that one
    Red seal.

That Would Be Scanned

The year started with poetry.
I scanned in whispers, catching
The rhythms of Hardy, Larkin.
Work out the beat; where lies the stress?
Would it be out by a foot, would we find
Curious aberrations to the rule?

Next, I was taught to scan
Documents and send them
Winging through digital air.
Mysterious message: picture and word.

Now, I'm the thing that is scanned.
My body the picture, mine the beat and the stress.
Curious aberration to the rule?
Ultrasound, CT, PET, Octreotide, MRI.

That almost scans.

Hepworth Haiku

Watch the spaces
In between –
Separating
Marbles,
Mother and child.

Villanelle In Jade

In ancient China, land of smoothest jade,
An emperor desired a goldfish bowl,
And he decreed of what it should be made.

His royal court, in silken robes arrayed,
Were told their lord desired a goldfish bowl
And that it should be formed of smoothest jade.

The task of carving this fine work was laid
Upon Li Chen, an artist, and his soul
Flared at the thought of goldfish bowl in jade.

His master's wishes had to be obeyed.
The piece of jade he carved from must be whole.
If he should fail, his lord would be betrayed.

While others searched for jade, the artist stayed
Designing a most lovely goldfish bowl,
And asked himself how much he would be paid.

Nine moons passed by before it had been made –
The smoothly-carved imperial goldfish bowl.
His master gasped; the smile began to fade:

'But goldfish can't be seen through walls of jade!'

Love Song To His Mobile

(with apologies to Henry Constable)

Heigho! How I do love thee.
I do love thee come the hour
Thou'rt charged with new life-giving power.
I feel thy smooth anatomy –
Thy sleek slim angularity.
I stroke thy screen, which will (I know)
Make thee respond and speak and glow
Under my touch – new warmth; a smear
From my lust-sweat. And now I hear
The outside world break in: a call!
You show me straight the name: I fall
Once more in love with she who rings;
Also with thee, who such joy brings.
Hello! How I do love thee.

Lunchtime Haiku

Blood transfusion. Peeled,
Split open, segments' veins are
Revealed.
Blood orange!

The First Duchess

The story of Kitty Pakenham, who in 1806 married the First Duke of Wellington.

I told him we should meet again.
Twenty-three when first I fell in
Love with him, he twenty-seven.

My father would not bless the match.
To prove his worth Arthur set sail
To India – Seringpatam;

Assaye; returned a hero; so
Yes, said father. April wedding
In the damp of Dublin city –

Dim as my eyes had grown. 'We must,'
I said, 'Meet just once more – once more
Before I walk the aisle.' How long

Since we last cast that loving glance?
Nine years.   I'd changed – knew I had changed.
The beauty Arthur caught in me

Had gone; the graceful liveliness
Gone too. But he cried 'No. No need
To meet. My feelings are unchanged.'

That glowering day, that gloomy
Church. I heard him murmur to his
Friend, 'Egad, she's ugly.' Ugly?

I hadn't thought he'd go that far.
We've done the best we can over
The years, the Duke and I. Victor

In Portugal and Spain, and then
The nation's feted darling
After Waterloo. No surprise

He liked to be with ladies full
Of wit and dazzle: how could I
Outshine Mrs. Arbuthnot? She

Who rattled about politics
To my Prime Minister husband?
Her nicknamed her 'La Tyranna'.

I stayed at Stratfield Saye, deep in
The folds of Hampshire; I brought up
Douro and Charles. Two sons I gave him.

'How long my nose is a-growing!'
Groaned his heir. He wanted that beak –
That eagle beak that pierced right through

Napoleon's dream. I couldn't
Manage the account books – feared
The reins of the house; cared only for

My children, and the servants,
And those who sheltered
Under my charitable care.

This angered the First Duke. His ire
Was also drawn by my grey hair,
My sad grey hair. 'Kitty, what you need

Is a wig.' As if he thought he stood
Addressing officers in the mess.
I bought a wig, and threw away

My battered straw hat. I'll admit –
Even my boys complained I dress
In a manner unbecoming.

Now clothes no longer matter. Here
I lie in Apsley House. The mob
Outside cares not at all that I

Am dying now. As my life thins
I hear the stones – like cannon balls –
They throw at our windows, enraged

That Waterloo's hero cannot
Abide Reform. He's by me now.
I place my hand around his arm;

Feel for the place. There! There it is:
The amulet I gave him when
We loved – young and ordinary.

I find it there, my proof of love –
And his: he loves me still. I touch
The hard, warm circle round his wrist.

Hearing It For The First Time

Black raincoat forgotten on the desk;
Suddenly bright June flowers, vivid by the path back home.
The curtains he pulled closed against the day;
Gothic-arched sofa; his hands checking the damage.

Back in the classroom – how do we know
What we think we know? That shirt –
Red and blue stripes gloriously present.
Was there ever in the world such a beautiful shirt?

It's A Swinging Life!

Come on a windy night and you'll find me
Slammed against my mate. We are
Inseparable.
In cracked duet
We creak, the gust tugging our chains,
Rocked, ridden by unseen ghosts.

Daytimes, I'm busy, dizzy sometimes
Watching the roundabout whirl; steadied
When mothers push
Small children who
Can't be left alone, in rhythmic motion
As if tilting them to settled sleep.

Ten year olds jostle, shove, reclaim me,
Their light seats scarcely touching mine
As they fly
High, up high,
Their voices shrill with the thrill that spreads before them
As they sense the giddying soar of their life ahead.

Evening falls, and we shudder, awaiting
A lurching battery – bottles and boys,
Crueller, clumsier
Than the wind.
As I groan under a bloated weight,
His girlfriend fixes her lipstick astride my mate.

We Know The Light Is There

Candles in daylight –
Why do we love you?
   Flames scarcely visible,
   A shuddering star
   That might next moment
      Die: we cannot
         Know.

When we let the match
Linger long as it kisses
   The lonely wick,
Until suddenly, silently
   A flame is alive
      And dancing,
         Then

We celebrate – that birth,
The simple fact we're here,
   Sharing time together –
      An English June; sun
   Casting the window shape
      Onto the carpet
         Drowns

Candle's white flame.
But we made our quiet point,
Didn't we? No need to wait for
Darkness, death's-head darkness
   Before we create the light.
      Our daytime candle
         Flame

Is light always,
Life always,
Our consecration
Invisible, shivering
There
On that lonely wick

What To Predict

My phone keypad knows my life —
Knows it too well, and there again perhaps
Not quite well enough. It makes mistakes.

Who is on what? Anthony on the radio
While I'm on radiotherapy? Why not
Reverse the guess? Do I want it to

Default to Interferon rather than interesting?
I admire the jump from carcinoid to
Crisis — although that sequence terrifies.

It knows that Adam's goes with
Graduation. It knows that York must
Follow. But no — I don't want it

To take me to hospital. I'll fight back.
Let's call it my Chelsea hotel.
Remember, phone. Chelsea HOTEL.

Written at The Royal Marsden Hospital, Chelsea

19

Advice

If your friend is ill…

And more especially
If they're in hospital:
Send a card they'll enjoy
Looking at from their bed.
Emails and texts should be
Short – just showing you care
And are thinking of them.
Never ever frame them
As a question. Replies
Are not the pastime of
The sick, so don't make them
Feel they need to message
Back. Help them keep their strength
For things that matter, like
Eating. Remember here
That food is important,
Food is key, when you're ill.
The patient may feel sick
At the very idea –
Or, steroid-boosted, long
For feasts. Find out if they
Are on a special diet.
Never assume that grapes
Or chocolates are the treat
You bring when you visit:
Forbidden fruit, perhaps?
But do bring edible
Goodies – of the right sort.
Don't – an important rule –
Outstay your welcome.
Half an hour to an hour,

Perhaps? You can't tell from
The patient: on the road
To recovery, they'll
Jabber away, so pleased
To have company.
But if you could see through
That closed door when you've left,
You'd take a guilty gasp
At the sheer exhaustion
With which they sink back on
Their pillow. All too much.
Give them news and gossip,
But please don't be afraid
To ask about their health.
The sense that you've become
An object of fear, source
Of contamination –
There's nothing worse than this
For the sick; the feeling
That others simply squirm
In mute embarrassment.
Let's part with one final
Rule – another never
Ever: don't try to call
Their mobile – though you could
Text beforehand to check
If it's okay. What might
The patient be doing
When you ring? Enduring
Blood extraction, talking
To doctor, unplugging
The drip en route to the
Loo? So just think things through
And you'll be the perfect
Friend to the stalwart sick.

Jane Eyre Haiku

Blind, maimed, my man –
And I'm now in the money.
A husband? He's perfect

Mrs Mounter By Harold Gilman

My cup is empty. Didn't take my pill.
I need more tea then. Pour, please. Do you mind?
Today I ache; the room is brown and chill,
Save the bright splash of colour straight behind.
I've tied this scarf around my head to warm
Both ears and throat. The fingers in my lap
Feel cold and swollen. What I crave's a form
Of central hearing, ecstasy on tap –
But that's just crazy dreaming. Here I sit
And watch you slam the kettle on the gas.
This chair is yours, this cup, this jug now lit
By ceiling bulb that makes it glow: not brass,
But magic pitcher blazing, burning gold
To snatch my brown-cased bones from pain and cold.

Paul Gauguin: Au Café (Mme. Ginoux) 1888

(also known as Café at Arles)

My elbow's weight upon the table pressed
Makes me feel strong and calm; for I am sure
That all those blank-eyed men behind me – poor,
Half-drunk, half-sleeping sots, think I too rest
In senseless dreaming sludge. But I am dressed
In formal dark and white. And on the floor
A small cat watches, happily alone, each paw
Set firm, its haunches straight, its breast
Puffed out complacently. The smoky haze
Is like a cloudy screen which severs me
From their dull, doltish world. It is as dense,
As solid as the snooker balls. The days
Of my bold gaming drift off noiselessly.
I sit and almost smile at my good sense.

Perdita

(A Winter's Tale)

Unfitting here in gaudy palace halls,
Bohemia's princess, soon Bohemia's queen,
I see spring come, new peeled from soft-skinned skies,
And all those daffodils of March reflecting sun.
Sheep-shearing days return; now my heart yearns
For youthfulness that I have quite foregone,
Never to hand to children of my own.
The marbled stone of royal corridors
Feels hard and cold and dull beneath my feet,
Which at this time of year would dance unshod
Upon the giving grass.

                Why then should I
Not take just once again a strange disguise,
Steal from the town and, thirsty, drink a draught
Of my old home? In that most secret glass
I see the shepherd's cottage. I see you,
Yes, Doricles, as on that morning when,
Seeking a falcon, you found me. Caught fast,
I perch here, mute in cage. But now I dare
To be a swallow and to fly back home,
To see once more the place that was so fresh,
So green, so sweet until it all was cropped
By anger of a father.

                After that,
I journeyed to Sicilia where I learned
That fury among fathers is not rare.
A basilisk, it kills and turns to stone.
A statue for a mother! Must I then
Be in this death-in-life a stone, a slab

Of art, Bohemia's perfect queen? And so
My love will grow as cold, a deadened thing
And absent as my youth. A winter's tale
Is all I have to tell. The teller's name
Is Perdita. For I have lost it all:
Youth, love, true nature. Springtime green has drained
Into Bohemian hillsides; all is grey.
Perdita. Quite lost. My life has turned away.

Remembrance Day 2001

'I played Yum-Yum when I was here.'
The eyes glaze over: weak, moist, blue.
Today is dim but the past is clear.

He played Yum-Yum when he was here.
His friend over there was a school-maid too.
Today is dim but the past is clear.

The school had no girls when he was here.
The Housemaster's daughter was all that he knew.
He yearned from afar but he never got near.

Now it's co-ed, and in school plays here
Boys can be boys, and a female crew
Of singing starlets will croon in your ear.

The names of the fallen are read out here.
In the first eleven he played with two.
'Yes, one died at Arnhem, one in Tangiers.'

He gazes around at the stern chapel – here
Where he sat as a boy, poked into his pew.
The bugle's last post resounds in his ear.
'I played Yum-Yum when I was here.'

Conker

When I feel the conker in my pocket
I remember him. My fingers close round
Its smooth solidity. It was autumn
Then, a different autumn, but like this
One ripe with golden sunshine and its gifts.

Summer has hardened and packed tight inside
This dense, warm little parcel of the year.
And warmer still it grows in my pocket
As I fondle and turn it in the dark,
The dark resting place of my coat pocket.

So is a good life packed full of doing
That may grow warm with others, even when
The many years have turned, and darkness filled
Places where memory shone bright and strong.
I feel the conker and feel he is here.

Toad

Swerving to avoid that blob of shit,
I look again and see it's a disguise.
A dark brown toad squats on muscled haunches,
Lump of primordial clay tricked into shape.

His orange eyes are fierce. He doesn't like
My brazen gaze. But we don't swap looks.
He keeps staring hard away, far away
Into the ancient pit that moulded him.

Café Man

I see through steaming windows rain-pocked cars, hear
their wet wheels hiss
As I cradle this tea-warmed cup. More steam. Push back
sleeves. Take pen; stir sugar onto page.
From unseen tables crickets' chatter, cutlery clatter – I
barely hear.
Swill hot weak tea, relish like sun-warmed, mud-sweet
summer puddles.
Dead pigs fly from bacon-busy pans; damp wool halitosis
pricks the scent of failure.
I wish this pen stirred magic spells, ladled fat scoops of
juicy verse.

Jumper

He didn't fit inside his world – arms like apes', a burnt-
   burger brownish black.
But when he hid inside it, the warm softness was an old
   dog's that licked and muzzled him.
It gave him silence, locking him in soundless snowdrift dreams.
Beckoned to baby days, he sucked on its saliva-milky comfort.
Burying deep inside, he smelt his mother's laundered breasts.
It wishes to make him weep once more.

Twin Giants

(In March 2001, the Taliban destroyed with dynamite the Buddhas of Bamiyan in Afghanistan)

After the heavy silence, a breath suspended
Gasped in the valley.
Then earth erupted,
Kush shuddered, shook,
Shell-shocked, vanquished,
Its gashed flank bled.

Gigantic holiness exploded, sattva streamed
Down mountain's edge.
Lips of the tranquil smile, now blown apart,
Tumbled on hard, dry earth.
Those heavy-lidded eyes, crossed limbs,
Torn open, smashed to dust.

Twin Buddhas, squeezed dead in the fist,
Fanatic fist, killed by the cold, hard eye,
Found Nirvana as they seethed through air
Then slumped to rubble. Those pedestals
(Keenly offered, cash offered) stand empty
In Metropolitan halls.

The revolution of the world is half-way through
Its turning year. A bright gold morning
Smiles. September. Again the earth
Explodes.
The twin gods of the west
Bend at the knees
And crumble
Into dust.

A Cancer Patient Visits Auschwitz

So many ways of setting specific sorrow
    Against some monstrous tragedy.
Look on this map of Europe, where a stain's spreading
    Over its once safe towns and fields.
Over the white seeps grey, and where plague is most foul
    Blackest lesions have inked the land:
        Dark blots of death.

My body is a map when, on the screen, I see
    The grey and black seep steadily,
Relentlessly, into the white regions, once safe
    And strong and healthy. Long ago
I watched my baby grow on such a screen. I know
    We're all formed both of good and bad
        Mashed, botched and ditched.

Let us not be dazzled by the bright white acres;
    Let us not be blind to evil.
It metastasised from Oslo to Salonika,
    Its black cells rotting Poland's flesh.
My little grief is tiny in comparison. Just think:
    For each of us a railway line
        Stretches ahead.

Anatomage

The ladies love that man on the anatomage.
He is (you could say) the vrai fromage.
His nakedness arouses badinage
Among this blue-rinsed entourage.
His innards show a sublime montage
Of organs and – mes braves, courage! –
All key parts in this male garage.
Shall we ask the medics for a bit of triage?
No, let's just stay gazing and paying homage
To our man lying on the anatomage.

...And Lemons

Is this the only game you know?
In and out the shiny stores;
Up and down between the floors;
Watching, as the baubles glow?

Are these the only stars you seek –
The little things that line the shelves,
Bright robes in which to hide yourselves;
The plastered beam upon the cheek?

Cry, cry – for when you sit at home,
You quake, I know, in secret fear.
And when you lie in bed, he's near –
But oh, you think, I am alone.

Slide Back The Lid

How to show all that I feel for you?
I give you a box of crayons –
A wooden box, with slide-on lid.

You'll try out the crayons, learn their colours:
Blue for the sky and green for the grass.
The red one could be used for striking out

Mistakes. You will no doubt create
Beautiful pictures, write fine words,
And I will trace your lines in wonder.

They will be your playthings, these crayons,
And your faithful friends – mine too:
The stakes that bind us upright.

You will use them every day, press down
On those tips, which will break, of course,
And we'll sharpen them, whittle them down

Till they grow quite short. Some things
Increase with age. Crayons don't.
They shrink into stumps, their tips

Like the caps of thin wooden dwarves.
The red – your correcting colour – will
Lead the shrinkage; sky blue and grass green follow.

Till you're finally left with a handful of stubs,
The squibs of my gift. One day we'll have
An empty box, and the pictures you've made.

A Smell Of Shampoo

As I shuffle in for tea, I catch immediately
A power-granting clue: the scent of
Herbal Essences. He's been at my shampoo.

Why has my brother washed his hair tonight?
His hint to Mum – I listened in, of course –
Won't be home till late. So what's her name then?

Under Investigation

I don't need to know why
   The sky is blue.
No-one can tell me why
   I lie here now,
   Bed next to rooftop window,
Taking in the day
   That turns to evening as I watch.

Simply, I want sky, rooftop, world
   Shown me anew.
We need the transfiguration
   Of our puzzling lives
Into something fresh. A word sown
   Brings to startling ranks
A force that dazzles, puffing fire.

Draw me into your blue mystery –
   Our sky, our world.
Teach us how to live – never to strain
   Against this endless strangeness.

Food; Feet

One among many things I learned:
Underfed, and your ankles swell;
Steps up or down – a hobbling oldie,
Your thighs grow fat, leak fluid.

Think of the Yazidis in Iraq, fled
To the mountains, choosing life,
Needing food. They clamber onto
Those heights, and starving ankles puff.

Here in safe Chelsea, I walk slowly
Out of the park, watching my steps
On the ground, watching the little girl
Push her pink doll's chariot over the grass.

Metamorphosis

First came a fear of cats
and a passion for pink,
bright scarves at her breast.

Then her voice cracked
quite suddenly, on Tuesday.
She'd always been a chatterer

but now chatter became chirp,
throat squeezed to chirrup –
message missed by the children.

By Thursday, they noticed that
she'd shrunk; Friday found her
perched on the coat rack

camouflaged by the feather boa
Polly wore to the New Year's party.
Now, as vernal equinox approaches,

she bursts from the boa, feathers
fluttering, and she's smaller still,
but bright and blushing in her new

pink apron, and he remembers her
as she was when he first knew her –
that feathered haircut was in fashion

and she flew at him for their first embrace.
Now, terrified, he sees her fly
in circles round the hall, the chirp

grown shriller, her eyes sprung sideways.
When she spots him, she seems as startled
by him as he is by her. They stare

at one another; her new beak opens
to peck at the seed sown years ago.
Then she flies hard at the closed window.

Displayed In Chelsea

How nice for the dwellers of Chelsea,
For the tourists who visit in droves
To spot the odd hospital escapee
Whose aura of otherness behoves

The healthy, the fit and the smoking
To tread SW3 with more care,
To steer round the tube-up-nose bloke in
Luke's Gardens; the dame without her hair.

They've got used to the man on the drip,
Machine shunted across Fulham Road
Where he chills at the café and sips
On coffee and sunshine – unloads

That husk, ward-dried sense of himself.
Or they might just see me – and my pump
And bandage and cannula. Health
Can implode with that very first lump.

Written at The Royal Marsden Hospital, Chelsea

Death Of A Clarinet

Today I threw my clarinet away.
Its grain was like the faded coat
Of some sick black beast, its keys were blind:
Dulled, filmed, spent; fire and burnish quenched,
Its throat was silent, stilled through lack of use.
Where was that sensual longing
Turned by Mozart enchantments into sound?
I threw my clarinet away today.

The snap of key on hole, the cork muffling
Its fall, and cork on all those joints –
It's thinned in each place like an old man's skin.
I cannot twist the aching parts
Of this neglected body into place.
So instead I stroke the mouthpiece,
My finger catching where I used to chew.
My clarinet I threw away today.

No single reed will wake this silent form.
A box from some Paris workshop
Lies where it's slept for years in its grey bed,
The lining of a broken case,
Sides split, catch slipped. It hasn't made a sound
For forty years. Clarinets now
Aren't made of wood. Plastic is tough; endures.
Today I threw my clarinet away.

Why keep it? Who can bring it back to life?
It died so long ago, it needs
Simple burial in a rubbish sack.
Let's face the end of life. Once supple, we
Don't re-assemble any more
To be what once we were; the sounds we make
Aren't silken like Prokofiev's cat.
I threw my clarinet away today.

I will be now forever doing this,
I know, until my voice is dumb.
I'll never play my clarinet again.
I'll never read those books. Take them,
Give them to those you love; give them to those
You'll never know, before they fade
And fester, like this dying beast –
My clarinet I threw away today.

Full Moon And Little Jessica

... after Ted Hughes, and remembering Jess's childhood

A black winter night, and through cold panes suburbs are
    silently freezing –
And you watching.
Next door's cat slides, soft as fallen snow,
Past the window. Black trunks hide the fence
For which it crouches, to spring from hence.

Men are going home, and women, out there on
    southbound roads and train lines you can't see –
A long unspooling of London workers,
Blind, indifferent stream.

"It's a moony night," you observe.
The moon hangs full, its silver face bright – riposte to a
    sunny day
As you point, all logic.

Your Story

(Downsizing: December 2013)

Your life in a lorry –
And our black panic
Clambering over the past,
The bagged detritus:
Its indiscriminate maw

Churning the jetsam,
The now unloved
Outmoded dark wood,
Dark-stained duvets,
Obsolescent videos,

Which rolled and heaved
Beneath us. 'Stop!' you cried,
As my scrabbling foot plunged
In a chasm between cast-offs.

But I couldn't stop.
Couldn't stop myself
Weeping the loss of your past.
The stories, the songs –
'Annabel',
'I'm Going to Cry'.
Already crying.

And letters: later you told me
The loss – the one written back-
Wards, so you had to read it
In a mirror. The ones from me
You found, all of them,
A plastic bag of mother-love,
Pulled from oblivion.

Curious to see a life
Stuffed into carriers:
Sainsbury's – stories;
Lidl – letters.
Still the murdered words
Churn inside the lorry,
Chasm where the life
Once told
Tumbled, rolled,
Its knell tolled
Into oblivion.

'Stop!' you cried.
And so the past
Sinks deep into our dark.
Close the van door.
In my head I secrete
All that I love. Plunge
Foot forward into
Our future –

Northanger Abbey Haiku

Adolescent lesson:
He falls for you, as he sees
   You're besotted.

On The Downs Above Kingston

Pausing to perch on the usual stile,
I turn away from the usual view
That looks out into the far distance
Over curvaceous slopes – the Downs
Meandering above the valley,
The catch of chalk cliff, the cars visible
On road underneath. I know
Where it goes; bears them on to the sea
Travelling east under a wide sky.

No, I'm swivelled round, scanning
The left-hand view – straight
Up the hill, the grass close-nibbled
By sheep, by rabbits, where I drop my gaze
Into the field you do not cross
When flocks are grazing there.
The eye travels up to the
Close-in vista of a bumpy hill
And, beyond the field's end,
The dark clumps of trees.
This angle disappears into
Woodland. You do not know where
It leads to. Neither do I.

NHMD

Like the vertically toppling gravestones
I left behind in Prague's cemetery –
No time to say good-bye to those beneath –
We stagger, shoulders crashing together,
In the cattle truck. I try to hold you
As close as I can to the barred window:
Fresh air. Breathe, little one, breathe this dark day
And many more to come. Please sir – I know
It's hard – you're feeling worse than I am now –
But try not to vomit on my baby.
I clutch her tight, side-stepping a puddle.

★

I'm here; now. Holocaust Memorial Day.
My children are alive. They came with me
To hear the poem read aloud – the one
I wrote for you and Ruth. I tried
To make it real – you clutching the baby
As, together, you took that final walk
Into the chamber. Strange word. That chamber
Wasn't bridal. A chamber of horrors:
Stationary cattle truck with no air –
Only the deathly stench, the gas that laid
Its pall over these past seventy years.
We each light a candle and clutch a stone.
The altar floor is shimmering with stones.
We are far now from that cemetery.
    We lay the stones down.

Birds And People

When I see a gull,
Its eye hard,
      Grey,
         Cold
            Still,
Its greedy beak slashing
Into rubbish sacks,
Its military feet pounding the grass
To make the poor worms rise,
I whisper that birds come lovelier in groups:

A flock of seagulls wheeling above the beach,
Their cry telling us to rejoice
In sky wide open, endless,
Their wings glinting sunlight;
A skein of starlings hovering like gnats
Ethereal in sunset above
The West Pier,
A delicate pouch of speckles.

And again I whisper

With people it's the other way round:
We come lovelier singly:
A man walks on the beach;
A child looks up at the fading sky,

Astonished;
Octogenarian pumps his stick, rising
From promenade bench.

Put them in a crowd –
They're ugly predators.
Put them in a crowd
And they march,

            Destroy.

Peel It...Away

Peeler – how I love to touch you:
To hold you tight in my right hand,
My index finger snuggling soft
Into that smooth, thoughtful indent,
Ring and baby digits curling
Into the handle's oval hole.

Peeler – you are my stainless steel
Rubber-legged cat. From your hard head,
Your silver triangular head
With its elegant neck, its hole
Round as a mouth licking fur,
Your dainty ears spring. Between ears

The sharp bite, the scratch, the quiet hiss
Cut straight across. This is my thrust
As I dig in – firm; strong;
Glide gloriously down
A comical carrot,
Your feline claw scraping,
Teeth stripping – till
The victim lies
Bare,
Flayed
  Skin
   Like
    Shreds
     Of
      Light.

On The Golan Heights

'They're in dry dock, you could say.'
Silent under their secret shroud
Hunch the tanks, the missiles, weapons

Alert for attack. In the next field
Hang bright globes, oranges
Waiting in groves to be ripe.

Spider

In dark and quick pursuit he'd been,
That scuttling devil, dancing up
To check. Afraid of him? Not me.
And no intent of mashing him.

Swift as the blow of bad news, he
Raced a length of skirting-board,
Then stopped suddenly, splayed legs wide.
Morning; open the bedroom door;

There he waited for me – silent,
Patient, his smile invisible:
He knew he'd catch me up; he knew.
Legs tautened, he'd climbed up the wall.

That's where I saw him last. We stared
Across the void at each other.
The void, he promised me, was dark,
As shit-dark as he. As for me –
I still refused to be afraid.

The Bee And The Snowdrop

(with a bow to Robert Frost)

Mild February days:
Spring sidles up to us,
Impatient impresario.
In the roadside lane the snowdrop bows
To passers-by, her multi-visored cap
Demure, screening her virgin secrets.

Here's one who would explore –
Penetrate
Rifle
That hidden chamber.
With clever limbs he clings
To her stem, and his dangerous fluff
Beckons in soft, striped splendour.

Invasive bumble bee,
As insistent as this spring day
Where you're a stranger;
You look so fatly misplaced there
On that delicate green stalk,
An anachronism that strayed,
Bold, premature, into February
Whose frosts may still you – suddenly -
Advanced so far from summer.

On the other side of the world
The polar icecaps melt.
Still the bumble bee holds fast
To this white maiden of spring.

February 1998

The Blossom Falls

Standing at the centre of my gaze,
    Insistent,
It was there each time I glanced up from my book --
   The bright white tree.
It beat at the very heart of the window
   With proud, independent pulse
(For it was outside, always outside,
   And never within me).
Loud, it mastered the hot green lawn.

   May blossom tree –
   Emblem of a lustless fertility,
Child of cold mornings early in spring
When pollen floats sadly about the wind's shoulder.
And now, whenever I looked up, unthinking,
The vision exploded once more to my eyes –
   Arrogant in its virginity,
   Extravagant in its purity.
Finally, transfixed there, I sat through the spell.

★

   I walk along the road,
   And the wind is blowing
   Blossom from the trees.
   Scraps of flickering white
   Drop noiselessly about me –
   Sometimes singly;
   Sometimes in crowds
   They fall.
   I know that wind, I think.

★

I looked out of the window suddenly.
I noticed a very ordinary green tree
    Flecked with dry brown.
     My proud tree,
   The garden's bright lady,
   Had been ravished
    Joylessly
By the blood-red tongue of time,
Which rolls round and round
    And round in its lapping.

     I admired you,
     Poor little tree,
     When you rose alone,
     Untouched by the garden,
     The child of unsinning.
     I resented you then –
     May I say it, my friend?
      I pity you now
     As you cringe at the sky
     And wither, absorbed
     In that stretch of rich grass.
     And your sadness is mine.
      Poor little tree.

Tu Bishvat Haiku

Tu Bishvat we plant trees–
Not for ourselves, but for
Our branches of young life.

Tuscan Garden

Stars still burn bright in the sky;
Fireflies flicker in the bush;
Invisible night-bird croaks.
We listen, watch; try to push

Into our nightfall – eclipse
Of that precarious spark.
They'll catch our breath as we slip
Into the taciturn dark.

Fireflies we wink off and on,
Plucking at those who pass by.
Night-bird croaks on from the tree;
Stars still burn bright in the sky.

The Albert Memorial

Pharaoh-like, golden, seated on a throne
Within that high pavilion wrought by hands
Heavy, Victorian (George Gilbert Scott),
The dead Consort surveys his dream: a land

Of learning – Albertopolis museums,
Offshoot of that other vision (crystal
Creation), British craft boasting to
Empire and world. Come, gaze at what we made.

Now, see that girl there on the grass in front
Of the memorial: striving almost
As Albert would have wished – trying hard
To do a handstand. Up; two seconds' thrust

And then she's down. So up again. A split
Second longer this time. Kicks up once more,
Straightens her legs; holds still; unfolds back down.
Try on! Cry of a dead Consort's stone lips.

Snowdrops Haiku

Maids demure, white tips to
Mob caps… Look now! They've
Splattered the lawn with snow

Tanka For Trevor

      Suddenly
    My puppy stops; pricks
Up ears; for now he smells, hears
     Winter's case breaking –
       Spring bursting.

Seaside Haiku

Low-slung dog on the
    Beach – a skittering crab in-
    hales Eternity.

Prayer

My father
Who healed the sick,
Now too far away
    To heal me,
Stir your spirit
    To remind me
What it is to live
The best that can be
    Lived
So long as I am
    Here.

Adar

Rosh Hodesh is the New Moon. Adar is the month in the (lunar) Hebrew calendar which signifies the start of spring.

Rosh Hodesh Adar – and you chose to die
On a day of bright sunlight when, as I
Turned the corner to where you lived, I saw
Snowdrops now jostled by slim crocuses

And daffodils. I rang the bell. Birds sang –
Your spring choir, choir of quittance. But inside
I found you did not seem to recognise
Our voices. You had set off already.

    Waiting to be
      Released,
    You lay in sun,
      Dazzled

    No longer. Breaths
      Came slow.
    We waited for
      The next –

    Which came. A gap.
      A breath.
    A greater gap.
      And then

    That last breath drawn,
      Waiting,
    We found it was
      The last.

What is death but another birth? A shift
Back to that unknown place we came from once.
You have taught me now how to fear it less.
Next it will be our turn; for now, we learn.

Funeral done,
    We drive
Under a clip
    Of moon.

An inverted
    Snowdrop –
It punches back
    The dark.

When it is a
    Quarter,
It will be your
    Birthday.

Now it blazons
    Out the
Re-birth of spring.
    Life! Life!

Links In The Bracelet

The surname has changed,
But the name you gave me
And the day I was given to you
    Remain the same.
This flimsy band on my wrist
So much larger than that first one,
The years so many in-between.
    This bracelet

Is a link between us, marking
A memory of that moment when
I moved outside you to enter your life.
    And the name
With the same initial letter that we share
Makes yet another link.
And so I carry on this spool,
    This bracelet.

I added a link and looked down at
Another tiny name band,
One with the same initial letter
    As yours and mine.

So the generations stretch on together,
Clasped in these bands of names
And in these bracelets of love
    Which move on
        Always forward
            Down the years.

Matrilineal

for Mum

You have never swerved
From your line of most resistance. Resist
Investigations,
Resuscitation,
Drugs that lure you back
Into a life you
No longer desire.

You do not resist
Lines you still must write –
Calling out at night,
Dictating from sleep
Those final letters
Of friendship and love.

What a gift for us –
Your words – spoken with
A smile, still bright-eyed:
'I have been so lucky.'

Since then, smile and eyes
Have faded, but still
You are majestic
As you sail into
Whatever happens:
You know we don't know.
Courageously, you
Face it, yearn for it.
You are showing us
The way. I thank you.

Daffodil Haiku

Mothers' Day daffs now
Drying in vase
Still glow – all
Buttery sunshine.

Snow Story

(For Susie)

They say
   It's not been heavier
      In eighteen years:
      This thickest snow
      Since your life began.

      Trace back
      Through the snow
And we suddenly see
      The two of us
Pushing up the hill,
      You in your buggy,
      Me trudging hard.

How short a childhood
      Between two snows.
      In raw winter sunshine
      The bundled baby –
Skin-bright, eye-bright
Seizing a blanched world –
Stood up and walked away
      Now visible
      Just
Moving, always moving
Through the departure gates
      Into the unknown

      While I trudge on
      Now downhill
      Through the snow.

Blind Man's Buff (Little Johnny-in-the-Wood)

Little Johnny-in-the-Wood
Stands blindfold.
Clutches air, mouthing.
Hordes seethe in, out, round.

His teeth gnash.
He bites out like
A madman. A beast.
Trees swing over, down, through.

Little Johnny-in-the Wood.
Stands snarling.
Lips lurch into a leer.
He senses the seething hordes but clutches only air.

He cries aloud.
Then slides into the
Plaintive moan of the lost.
He knows. Trees creak. He knows it is despair.

Little Johnny-in-the-Wood.
Howls in the horror.
Of loneliness. Howls
In the terror of recognition:

Someone has touched him.
And run away.
Someone
Burnt a hole
In the cloak of his night.
And then melted.
To the trees.